VULGAR VERSES

Collected by
Michael Rosen

Illustrated by
Riana Duncan

André Deutsch

First published in 1991 by
André Deutsch Limited
105–106 Great Russell Street, London WC1B 3LJ

Text copyright © 1991 by Michael Rosen
Illustrations copyright © 1991 by Riana Duncan

ISBN 0 233 98736 3

Typeset by AKM Associates (UK) Ltd,
Ajmal House, Hayes Road, Southall, London

Printed in Great Britain by
WBC, Bridgend

Foreword

In 1989 came 'Rude Rhymes', in 1990 it was 'Dirty Ditties' and now – volume three. There seems to be a never-ending stream (as the little boy said looking down at his . . .) and even as I write this, new rhymes are coming in. Yet I can't help thinking that we're probably only skimming the surface. The fact is, people in all walks of life invent and/or retell rude rhymes; and age is not barrier either – the age range of the collection is over eighty years, running from young children to a kind contributor of 88.

Another old chestnut pleasingly exploded is the one that says filth is a nasty male habit restricted to little boys, big boys and old boys. Not so. A quick glance down the names of people offering their rhymes will show that the habit is unisex. In fact, some of the offerings from young women were – well – extraordinary, including one who told me she composes them, at the drop of – er – a hat, and another who makes them up about men in the office concerning matters of size and performance. Perhaps there's scope here for a collection of Women's Workplace Wisdom, I thought.

Meanwhile, on the word-by-mouth front, all is well. Children go on producing parodies and jingles – look out for Kylie Minogue's 'I should be so lucky' and only the other day I was crossing a playground and children were singing:

> 'This is Margaret Thatcher
> Throw her up and catch her
> squishy squashy
> squishy squashy
> this is Margaret Thatcher'

The 'squishy squashy' bit was accompanied by the children grinding and squashing their hands together – presumably with Margaret Thatcher in the palms of their hands. Funny old world.

What of the future? Well, if the rhymes keep flooding in, then there's scope for a volume 4 – though I am beginning to run out of titles. Another possibility is a bumper volume of all three plus good extras, and the more I think about that Women's Workplace one, the more I like it: Office Offerings and Factory Filth? Send it all in to: Michael Rosen, c/o Andre Deutsch Ltd, 105–106 Great Russell Street, London WC1B 3LJ.

A clever commercial female
had prices tattooed to her tail.
And below her behind
for the sake of the blind
a duplicate version in braille.

Petra Hooks, 14
Reading

There was a young hooker from Crewe
who filled her vagina with glue.
She said with a grin
'If they pay to get in
they can pay to get out again too.'

Miss Debra Wride, 23
Birmingham

There was an old lady
who lived in a shoe,
she had no children
she knew what to do.

Dr Tim Healey, 55
Barnsley

Oh Gor Blimey, Mother can't find me,
under the table, playing with Mabel,
up goes the petticoat, down go the drawers,
my little winkle, just fits yours.

woman, 69
Chatham

I'm a little dutch boy,
I don't swear,
shit, bugger, arsehole,
I don't care.

Richard Griffiths, 25
from childhood, Beeston, Notts

I don't drink
I don't smoke
I don't swear
ah shit, I left my fags at the pub

Ritchie Shipton, 13
Herts

ADVERT

Use Ex-lax
to Re-lax
your bo-lax

Bryan H. Voyle, 44
Cornwall

Not last night, but the night before
three little monkeys came to the door.
One had a fiddle
one had a drum
one had pancake stuck to his bum.

Anne, 40; Eileen, 42; Jean, 30
Edinburgh

How do you tell a Scotman's clan?

Put your hand up his kilt and if he's got a
Quarterpounder
he's a Macdonald.

Chris Mangnall, 14
Lancashire

There once was a man called Reg
who got off with a girl in the hedge.
Along came his wife
with a carving knife,
and cut off his meat and two veg.

Kate Rosewell, 11
Bridgehampton, Somerset

There was a young man from Rangoon
who was born three months too soon.
He hadn't the luck
to be born with a fuck
He was scraped off the bed with a spoon.

Mrs F. Longson, 88
Derbyshire

There once was a man called Green
who invented a wanking machine.
His wife, she awoke
the fucking thing broke
and whipped his balls to cream.

Phil Goodwin, 26
Doncaster

There was an old man from Crocket
who went to the moon in a rocket.
The rocket went bang,
his balls went clang,
and his dick ended up in his pocket.

D. Pritchard, 31
learnt at 9
Accrington, Lancs

Down in the valley
where nobody goes
there's a big fat lady
without no clothes.

Down comes a cowboy
clippety clop
down with his trousers
and out with his cock.

Two months later
all was well
five months later
her belly did swell.

Nine months later
her belly went pop
out came the baby
with a paralysed cock.

Ladies and gentlemen
that's not all.
The poor little bugger
only had one ball.

girl, 13
London

'If skirts become much shorter,'
said the typist with a blush,
'there'll be two more cheeks to powder
and a lot more hair to brush.'

Dr Tim Healey, 55
Barnsley

I thought it'd be alright . . .

You know what Thought did, don't you? Followed a dung cart 'cos he thought it was a wedding; piddled in his pants 'cos he thought they weren't there . . .

man, 44
London

Roses are red
violets are blue
I'm in bed
where are you?

Nicola Best, 20
Wiltshire

There was an old woman
who lived in a bucket.
I had a good rhyme,
but Mum made me chuck it.

Dr Tim Healey, 55
Barnsley

I swear to God I love you,
I love you 'cos you're good.
You're good because God made you,
by God I wish I could.

Dr Tim Healey, 55
Barnsley

My girl sucked my willy
till it turned blue,
now it's shrivelled up
and looks like a shoe.

Jack Staples, 13
South London

The angle
of the dangle
is directly proportional
to the height of the shelf
the magazine came from.

boy, 15
Strathclyde

Long and thin, goes too far in
and does not please the ladies.
Short and thick just does the trick
and manufactures babies.

Anne, 40; Eileen, 42; Jean, 30
Edinburgh

The boy stood on the burning deck
his thing was covered in blisters.
The doctors came and cut it off
and now it's like his sister's.

Emma, 14
Dorset

If your mouth was an arsehole
and your arsehole was a mouth,
you'd be blowing shit out both ends
and yelling out your dick for help.

girl, 16
North Island, New Zealand

Old Mother Hubbard went to the cupboard
to fetch the postman a letter.
When she got there
the cupboard was bare
so they had it without – it was better.

Jonathan Nash, 21
Derbyshire

NOTICE SEEN ON A DIRECTOR'S DOOR

Never before in the whole of my life
have I ever met anyone with as many problems
and such bad luck as you have.
Your story has really touched my heart –
now piss off and stop bothering me.

Jonathan Nash, 21
Derbyshire

Riddle:

My Auntie Mary
has a thing hairy.
My Uncle John
has a thing long.
My Uncle John
put his thing long
into Auntie Mary's hairy.

What is it?
broom handle and broom.

Dr Tim Healey, 55
Barnsley

There once was a man from Brazil
who took an atomic pill.
His legs expired
his bum backfired
and his cock shot over the hill.

girl, 16
North Island, New Zealand

There was a young woman named Sally
who stripped at the working men's Palais
she got lots of applause
when she pulled down her drawers
'cos the hairs on her head didn't tally.

Barry Saunders, 31
Herts

Tune: 'My Bonny Lies over the Ocean'

My father's a lavatory cleaner
he cleans them by day and by night
and when he comes home of an evening
his shoes are all covered in . . .

shine up your buttons with Brasso
it's only thre'pence a tin,
you can buy it or nick it from Woolies
but I doubt they've got any in.

Some say he died of the fever
some say he died of the flu
but you and I know what he died of
he died of the smell of the . . .

shine up your button with Brasso
it's only thre'pence a tin.
You can buy it or nick it from Woolies
but I doubt they've got any in.

Some say he's buried in a graveyard
some say he's buried in a pit.
But you and I know what he's buried in.
He's buried in six foot of . . .

shine up your buttons with Brasso
it's only thre'pence a tin.
You can buy it or nick it from Woolies
but I doubt they've got any in.

Jamie Butler, 26
Merseyside

Sung: 'My Old Man's a Dustman'

My old man's a dustman
he wears a dustman's hat
he took me round the corner
to watch a football match.

Fatty passed to Skinny,
Skinny passed it back.
Fatty took a rotten shot
and knocked the goalie flat.

Where was the goalie
when the ball was in the net?
Halfway round the goalpost
with his knickers round his neck.

They put him on a stretcher
they put him on a bed
along came a little dog
and piddled on his head.

Kirsty Sloman, 19; Russell Couper, 19
Cornwall

Dan, Dan the sanitary man
Superintendent-General of the lavatory pan.
He puts in the paper
and changes the towels
works to the rhythm of the rumbling bowels.

Carolyn Skudder, 30
Devon

DIRTY DEFINITIONS

Innocence:
nuns doing press-ups in a cucumber field.

Russell Wernham, 16
Berks

Agony:
Horse in a wet suit having an erection.

Frustration:
One-armed bandit hanging off a cliff with itchy balls.

Louise Davies-Jones, 17, Bristol; Andrew Drury, 13,
Derby

A bum:
Kojak with a splitting headache.

boy, 9
London

Impossibility:
trying to pin diarrhoea to the wall.

Kate Lawrie, 18 and sister, 19
Bucks

A prostitute is like a police station:
Dicks going in and out.

D.R. Freeman, 41
Surrey

A drawing pin:
A Smartie with an erection.

A snail:
a bogy with a crash helmet.

girl, 11
Brill, Bucks

Proverb

A bird in the hand . . . does it on your wrist.

boy, 17 and girl, 13
Surrey

The world is full of feather beds
and little girls with curly heads.
So really there is no excuse,
for sodomy and self-abuse.

Dr Tim Healey, 55
Barnsley

Jack be nimble
Jack be quick
Jack jump over the candlestick;
silly boy
should have jumped higher
goodness gracious!
Great balls of fire!

boy, 16
Cairo, Egypt

Kids in the front seat cause accidents.
Accidents in the back seat cause kids.

So don't buy a car with a backseat,
so sperms will never roam
because no lady's legs will be home.

girl, 16
North Island, New Zealand

Roses are red
Violets are blue
. . . hanging on next door's line.

Dr Tim Healey, 55
Barnsely

Are you coming?
No, it's just the way my trousers hang.

man, 44
London

Wouldn't it, wouldn't it
wouldn't it be funny
if a lady had a wooden tit
wouldn't it be funny?

Carolyn Skudder, 30
Devon

(Harlem, New York skipping song)

Kiss my acker-backer
my soda cracker
my B,U,T
my doodie-hole
your ma
your pa
your greasy granny
wears dirty panties
gotta big behind
like Frankenstein
gotta root-toot-toot
like a prostitute
gotta ding dong
like King Kong
gotta beat-beat
on Sesame Street.

Karol Swanson
South Queensferry, Scotland

Abraham Lincoln was a very good man,
he jumped out the window with his dick in his hand.
He said, 'Excuse me, ladies, I'm just doing my duty,
now pull down your pants and gimme some booty!'

Joe Sender, 11
London

Tune: 'Oh dear what can the matter be?'

Oh dear what can the matter be?
Three old ladies stuck in the lavatory,
they've been there from Monday to Saturday
nobody knew they were there.

The first was called Elizabeth Porter
went there to get rid of some unwanted water.
The second was called Elizabeth Humphrey
who sat on the lav and couldn't get her bum free.
The third was called Elizabeth List
went in with a bottle and came out pissed.

Katie, 12
Clwyd

Sung, tune: 'The Old Grey Mare'

The old black bull said,
'Let's have anothery
down by the shrubbery,
you bring the rubbery.'

The old brown cow said,
'You can go to buggery
I ain't gonna do it no more.'

John, 28 and Linda 25, Motyka
Melbourne, Australia

Sung: 'Half a pound of Tuppenny Rice'

Half a pound of Mandy Rice
half a pound of Keeler,
neither girl is very nice,
everybody feel her.

Dr Tim Healey, 55
Barnsley

As I was walking down the town
I saw two people lying down.
Her skirt was up,
his arse was bare
I saw the flesh beneath the hair.
His balls they twangled to and fro
if that's not fucking, I don't know.

Anne, 40; Eileen, 42; Jean, 30
Edinburgh

How do you do it?
Putting on a 'Joe'.
It takes me an hour to put it on
and all she wants is a blow.

girl, 16
North Island, New Zealand

When you get married
and you have twins,
don't come to me
for safety pins.

Ghisleine Quinn, 15
Stockport

Have you ever caught your dick in a mangle,
when some bloody fool turns the handle?
Your nuts go crack,
your dick flips back,
have you ever caught your dick in a mangle?

Carla Holden, 15
Cumbria

The boy stood on the burning deck
and wondered why he'd been born.
His father said, 'You wouldn't have been
if the Durex hadn't torn.'

Katie, 12
Clwyd

FUZZY DUCK (Game for more than four,
preferably when some or all are drunk:)

Sit in a ring and first person says: 'To my left fuzzy
duck' so the person on the left has to say: 'To my left
fuzzy duck' and so on round the ring until someone,
(anyone) says 'Does he?' then back goes the phrase
but this time as 'To my right ducky fuzz'. When
someone says 'Does he?' change direction again and
go back to 'To my left fuzzy duck'.

Whoever says: 'Duzzy fuck' or 'Fucky duzz' pays
a penalty (?!) and that person has to restart the game.

boy, 15
Strathclyde

Jack McGrew was five foot two,
and hated the way he was built,
'cos dogs would follow him all around
and sniff right up his kilt.

Barry Saunders, 31
Herts

Sung: My little pony tune

My little pony
skinny and bony
born in a stable
drinking Black Label
that stupid swine
cost 5.99

Abigail Kristy Silvester, 12
London

I wish I were a caterpillar
for life would be a farce.
I'd climb up all the buds and trees
and slide down on my . . . hands and knees.

Dr Tim Healey, 55
Barnsley

Do not blame poor doggy,
it's not his fault at all.
Someone left a wet umbrella
hanging in the hall.

Dr Tim Healey, 55
Barnsley

Needing to go to the loo by Ivor Poo, Willie Makit, Betty Wont

Andrew Drury, 13
Derby

Wanking by Paul Backskin

Boy, 14
London

Bubbles in the Bath by Ivor Wynn D. Bottom

boy, 17 and girl, 13, Surrey; man, 53, Calgary, Canada

The Cat's Revenge by Claud Balls

man, 53, Calgary, Canada

Sung, tune: 'Old Smokey'

On top of old Smokey
all covered in grass,
a bald-headed eagle
sat scratching its . . .

Now don't get mistaken
and don't get misled,
that bald-headed eagle
was scratching its head.

Kate Lawrie, 18 and sister, 19
Bucks

Sung: 'I should be so lucky'

I should be so lucky
with my rubber ducky
strangle Mrs Mangle too.
Steph'nie had a baby
called it Stupid Jamie
and that's the end of Neighbours too.

girl, 6
London

Sex is an evil
evil is a sin.
Sin is forgivable
so get stuck in.

Adam Prout, 15
London

A sexy PT teacher had a voice both loud and rasping.
And when she'd finished with the boys
they were on their knees and gasping.

Barry Saunders, 31
Herts

I asked, how come the wind blows?
God said, fuck knows.

girl, 13
Bucks

Titsaleena Bumsquirt Big Banana Feet
went to the pictures and fell through the seat.
When the picture started
Titsaleena farted
Titsaleena Bumsquirt Big Banana Feet

Ian Hodgkinson, 14
Arizona, USA

Tune: 'These Foolish Things'

A sweaty sock beside an old french letter
a dose of syphilis that won't get better
my foreskin stings and all these things
remind me of you.

A pair of testicles with lipstick traces
the night you caught your tits in my new braces
my foreskin stings and all these things
remind me of you.

G. Crawford, 20-ish
Lincoln

Sung:

I'm a little tea-pot
short and silly.
Here's my handle
here's my willy.
When the tea is ready
hear me hiss.
Lift me up
and see me piss.

man, 44
London

Sung: 'Kookaburra Sits in the Old Gum Tree'

Kookaburra sitting on the hot tin wire
jumping up and down with his bum on fire.
Scream kookaburra, scream
how hot your arse must be.

Louise Davies-Jones, 17
Bristol

DIRTY BOOKS

'Nail on the Bannister' by R. Stornaway

'Piddle on the Bathroom Floor' by I.P. Squint

Anne, 40; Eileen, 42; Jean, 30
Edinburgh

Yellow River by I.P. Daily

Baby's Revenge by Nora Titoff

John, 28 and Linda, 25, Motyka
Melbourne, Australia

I'm not a pleasant pheasant plucker
I'm a pleasant pheasant plucker's son
and I'll go out plucking pleasant pheasants
till my pleasant pheasant plucking days are done.

Anne, 40; Eileen, 42; Jean, 30
Edinburgh

The doggies held a conference
they came from near and far.
Some of them came by aeroplane
and some by motor car.

As each doggy queued
to see the visitor's book,
each doggy took its arsehole off
and hung it on a hook.

As they were assembled
each pure breed dam and sire,
some dirty rotten bastard
came in and shouted, 'FIRE!'

The dogs were in a panic,
they had no time to look,
so each dog grabbed an arsehole
off the nearest hook.

And that is why you'll see today
a dog will leave a bone
to sniff another's arsehole
to see if it's their own.

Gareth Jackson, 14
Stockport

Note left by bride, pinned to pillow.

The shoehorn's on the mantelpiece
the vaseline's on the shelf.
I saw that great big thing of yours,
so I chloroformed myself.

Dr Tim Healey, 55
Barnsley

A rooster says cock-doodle-do.
A prostitute says, any cock'll do.

John, 28 and Linda, 25 Motyka
Melbourne, Australia

Molly owned a shellfish stall
She'd serve you in a twinkle
And if you didn't know the way,
she'd soon fish out your winkle.

Barry Saunders, 31
Herts

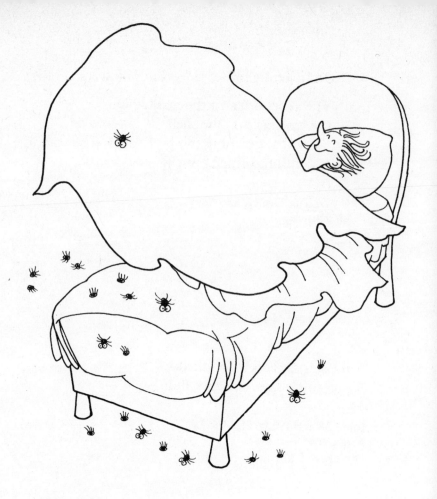

A sigh is but a puff of wind
coming from the heart,
if it should take a downward course
it's often called a fart.

To fart it gives you pleasure
it gives the bowels ease.
It warms and airs the blankets
and drives away the fleas.

Mrs A. Smith, 40
Surrey

Newspaper headline:

LADY TRUCKDRIVER SWERVES TO AVOID
CHILD
– and falls out of bed.

Dr Tim Healey, 55
Barnsley

There was an old fakir of India
who thought of a wonderful trick,
he greased his arsehole with butter
and slowly inserted his prick.
It wasn't for fame or fortune
or any fabulous wealth.
It was just to please an old comrade
who told him to fuck himself.

man, 70
London

Toilet graffito:

It's no use standing on the seat,
the crabs in here can jump six feet.

Dr Tim Healey, 55
Barnsley

WRITTEN ON LOO WALL

If in this bog there is no paper
under the seat you'll find a scraper.
If the scraper cannot be found
drag your arse across the ground.

Chris Mangnall, 14
Lancashire

I kissed her lips
while making passes,
She closed her legs
and broke my glasses

girl, 14
London

Watership Down
you've read the book,
you've seen the film
– now eat the pie.

boy, 17 and girl, 13
Surrey

It's better to fart and stink a little
than keep it in and be a cripple.

Angela, 32 and Jason Ward, 10
Dyfed, Wales

Fatty and Skinny went to the zoo
Skinny got stuck in some elephant's poo.

Michael Rockwell, 19
Inverness

Be ozone friendly –
fart in a bottle!

J. Dent, 20
Norwich

Fatty and Skinny were in the bath
Fatty farted and Skinny laughed.

Kate Angel, 21
London

If you suck my tits
I'll suck your bits.

girls, 13
Isle of Wight

You start as somebody's sperms
end, being eaten by worms.
And the part in between
is, as you've seen
full of diseases and germs.

Terry Cuthbert, 43
Oxford

There was an old man called Jock
who had a fifty foot cock.
It hit a tree
and he pissed on a flea
and twisted it round a rock.

Terence Chambers, 13
Lincs

LATIN

Boyibus kissibus
sweet girliorum
girlibus likibus
wanti sumorum.

Dr Tim Healey, 55
Barnsley

How's your bum for lovebites?
Alright, on the whole.

Gabi Parsons, 26
Bucks

There was a cow stood in a field,
silly cow she wouldn't yield.
The reason why she wouldn't yield,
she didn't like her udders feeled

Barry Saunders, 31
Herts

Graffiti in a public lavatory:

Don't throw your fag ends in the loo
you know it isn't right.
It makes them very soggy
and impossible to light.

boy, 17 and girl, 13
Surrey

Sign in a railway station:

Toilets out of order,
please use platforms 5 and 6.

boy, 17, and girl, 13
Surrey

WRITTEN ON A TOILET WALL

If you sprinkle
while you twinkle
be discreet
and wipe the seat.

Petra Hooks, 14
Reading

Here's to the game of twenty toes,
It's played all over the town,
The girls play it with ten toes up,
The boys with ten toes down.

David Morris
Birmingham

I lost my leg in the army
I lost my leg in the navy
I lost my cock in the butcher's shop
and I found it in the gravy.

Anne, 40; Eileen, 42; Jean 30
Edinburgh

How is sex like maths?

Subtract clothes
add bed
divide legs
and multiply.

boy, 15
Strathclyde

Success:
Two gays walking down the street with a pram

Pain:
Sliding down a razor blade using your balls as
stoppers

girl, 13
Bucks

A bra:
Over the shoulder boulder holder
Upper decker flopper stopper.

A jock strap:
Lower decker knacker jacket.

Mrs Holmes, from 1970s
Fareham, Hants

The owl and the pussycat went to sea
in a beautiful pea-green boat.
The pussycat's pee was greener still
and kept them both afloat.

children, 5
Hammersmith, London

What's pink and hangs out your boxer shorts?
Your mum on washing day.

boy, 15
Strathclyde

Here I sit as bored as hell
waiting for the fucking bell.

Kate Lawrie, 18 and sister, 19
Bucks